Protecting Your Peace by Any Means Necessary

By. Jerrell A. Gooden

DEDICATION

THIS BOOK IS DEDICATED TO HATTIE MAE DRAKE
GOODEN
A LOVING MOTHER, SISTER, AUNT, GRANDMOTHER

CONTENTS

PREFACE

This book will be about maintaining your peace and not letting anybody or anything disturb it. When you want peace in life, you cannot be the cause of the chaos. I will be talking about how to keep the peace and be respectful to others in the process because we are all trying to strive for certain goals, but your mind must be at peace for your dreams to come true.

There will be some things that will be talked about on how your peace can be disrupted or destroyed, and there will be some solutions on how to have a peaceful life and keep it that way. Peace is one of the most important assets to have when living life to the fullest. Protecting your peace is very important. There are many ways that I will be talking about how you can protect your peace; there will be some stories that will be used as examples and everything.

When you have peace of mind you can do anything that you set your mind to. Positive thinking will play an important part in maintaining a sane mind. It can be hard to live in peace sometimes, and that will also be disgust in this book because I feel that peace can be a challenge when you are around the wrong crowd. Life is hard enough as it is, and the last thing you want to lose is your peace.

I am not an expert on any of this that I am about to talk about in this book, but I can give some of the best advice coming from my personal experiences that I have encountered in life. Well, I hope whoever is reading this book will enjoy it and get something out of it.

Remember, never let anyone or anything destroy your happiness or your peace. The devil will send his followers out to do just that because certain people do not want to see you either happy or doing better than them. Praise God in the good and bad times because life is too short not to be happy, and you should have a sound and open mind about things that may happen unexpectedly.

CHAPTER 1

What is the Meaning of the Word Peace

THE true meaning of the word peace is defined as societal friendship and harmony in the absence of hostility and violence. In a social sense, peace is commonly used to mean a lack of conflict (such as war) and freedom from fear of violence between individuals or groups. Another definition of the word peace can also mean freedom from disturbance, and tranquility.

In this chapter, I will be discussing the meaning of the word peace in my own words. The word peace means that you are not bothered by what is or may be going on around you; it is just like being a kid all over again without a care in the world just living life and enjoying the good times that you may be having as a child. Sometimes, I wish that I was still a kid that can just live life and do what my parents told me to do and that would be it.

The word peace can mean a lot of things; it also depends on the individual as well as how they may interpret the word in their meaning. I

personally hate it when my peace is either

disrupted or disturbed because it can ruin my

whole mood for the entire day for example

sometimes when I was getting ready for school as

a child, my mother nagged and fussed at me in the

morning, especially on some of their day that I

didn't do anything wrong however, my mother

would tell me that when you have kids of your own

one day, then you will understand.

Being at peace with yourself is a very

important mindset to have because, without inner

peace, you will either be mad all the time or lose

your sanity. When you have that inner peace with

yourself, you will be in a different mindset and your

brain will be cleared of all distractions that may be a nuisance to you. It is just life when someone comes to you gossiping about someone else's business that do not concern either you or that person who may be talking to you about their situation. Do not get me wrong I am not perfect when it comes to talking about certain people; I mean we are all guilty of it now and then, but you also have certain people who thrive so much off drama that it comes to the point that you hate to see them coming with some unnecessary stuff that is destroying your peace. The people who thrive on drama and keeping negative energy going, they either do not have and life of their own or are miserable with themselves on the inside.

Protecting Your Peace by Any Means Necessary

I told myself a long time ago that I am going to protect my peace no matter what. Peace can also mean a relationship of living well together. You can and will have more peace when you are around individuals that want the same thing as far as having a clear mindset about life especially when you have that life partner that is going to make sure that you are alright with certain things that may be going on in the relationship and vice versa.

It is not always going to be easy to live and maintain your peace all the time. We are going to have moments when our peace will be put to the test; it is just like following God and doing his will which is in heaven I mean that is not easy by any means daily. I know that I fall short each day, but if I have a breath in my body and can wake up every

morning and repent and thank God for the day that

has given me, then there is always and chance to

get it right and make peace not only with yourself

but with the good Lord Jesus Christ as well.

Remember to always trust God in every situation

no matter how bad things get. He is always in

control of everything.

CHAPTER 2

Learning How to Say the Word NO

When maintaining and keeping your peace intact, I honestly believe that you must learn how to say the word NO. Some people have a hard time doing just that for numerous reasons. I had to learn at a young age because when you start to become a yes man, then it is only a matter of time before no good people will pray on your weakness and take advantage of you. I may get used once, but I refuse to let it happen twice, especially by the same person.

We must learn that some people have an alternate motive when it comes to taking advantage of you. Some people can see other people's bad intentions coming from a mile away however, it takes some time for others to realize that they are being used and being taken advantage of. The people who may be reading this chapter may be asking themselves what phase of learning how to say the word no has to do with maintaining your peace; well, I as the author of this book will tell you. When you start and learn how to say the word no, you are protecting your peace because when you just say yes to anything, it can get you into messed up situations that you may have a hard time getting out of.

There are reasons why people say the word no to protect their peace. One reason would be is that they may not feel comfortable doing certain things for example speaking in front of people in class. I remember when I was in college and I had the speech class that I had to pass for me to get my degree; I didn't feel comfortable at all giving a speech, but I knew that it had to be done. Sometimes, we must step out of our comfort zone from time to time.

It is also important to follow your gut feeling because most of the time your inner self is right. We all have that inner voice that tells us when to do something or just leave the situation alone all together. Saying no can be hard sometimes especially when you are used to saying the word yes to people just to maintain either an image or friendship. You cannot say the word yes, all the time because it can get you into trouble. The last thing you want to be labeled as is a yes man or woman. Some people may know that they are getting taken advantage of, but their hearts are so good that they feel like they are going to lose important people in their lives by saying the word no.

When you are a yes man and people know it, they expect you to jump through hoops (metaphorically speaking of course) for them and be there every time they need but cannot get the same thing in return. The moment you start saying the word no, then your circle of so-called friends starts to get smaller. You really find out who your real friends are when you start denying then easy access to you all the time.

Some people will also try to throw things in your face when you finally put your foot down and tell them off. We must learn to protect our peace by any means because some people in this world are playing for keeps and leaving you high and dry when you are no longer necessary in their lives.

Other people will also try to say that you have never done anything for them the moment you say the word no. Gaslighting is very real in this world, and it is up to us to be on the lookout on how people really are when either times get hard or you just had enough of somebody that always have their hand out and do not have anything to offer in return as soon as you get done helping them. I personally try to stay away from people that are always complaining about little things or just so negative about everything.

You may hurt some people's feeling you finally say that you had enough, but in the long run you will still maintain your peace and have a clear mind on things. All I am saying is to keep an open mind about the true intentions of certain people. When it comes to keeping your peace, you may have to hurt people's feelings when you say the word no because there is a word that is called self-preservation.

CHAPTER 3

Never Take Everything to Heart

Taking everything that anyone says to you personally can be your downfall when it comes to maintaining your peace of mind. I personally sometimes take things to heart too much myself, however as the years have gone by, I learned that people may be either joking or just ribbing me from time to time. My late mother always taught me not to take things to heart all the time.

Jerrell A. Gooden

I honest feel that we must have some fun out of life instead of taking everything so seriously all the time. It is just like being in a relationship with someone; when one or both parties take things so seriously all the time, then the relationship will not be a good one. I had to just let go and enjoy life a little more on a personal level. I had to do a self-evaluation on me and try to figure out why am I taking what people say so personal when I shouldn't have to. The reason why I did a self-evaluation on myself was because the things that I was stressing about was interfering with my peace of mind. It is important to not take things to heart all the time because it is like I said before, some people do not mean any harm or disrespect all the time.

Protecting Your Peace by Any Means Necessary

Sometimes in life, it is less important to be
right than it is to be at peace because as we get
older, we really do not have the time nor the energy
to argue with a person who feels like they are right
all the time and cannot do any wrong. I recall when
I was younger, I would cry a lot as a little kid
because any little thing that was said to me out of
the way would just set me off into tears. I have
been insulted throughout my life and the perfect
example of that would be that I was told that I
would never be in a relationship because I am not
thug enough and too nice; that had me in my
feelings so bad that I went to Facebook and talked
about it. I know that it was wrong for me to do but
at the same time, I had no one that would listen to
me about my problems at the time. I few days later

the same girl that insulted me said that we were

beefing and to be honest I did not care because I

felt that she should have not said what she said

when she insulted me; and another girl had the

nerve to tell me that I need to go and apologize for

what I said about her on social media and to be

honest it felt like I didn't owe her one because she

was the one that insulted me. I took it personally

because of what I have been through in the past

and when she said what she said to me, it did

nothing but create personal flashbacks that I do not

want to relive repeatedly.

Another way to not take things so personally

is to let things go that have been bothering you

over the years. Letting the past go based on how

you may have been treated can be a tall order. You

vividly remember the things that a person may have said or done to you that you may have not agreed with. From my personal experiences in life, it is hard not to hold grudges towards people that either mistreated or just was using you for their gain.

Holding on to an old grudge will not do anything except cause you more grief. That is why each day it is important for us to pray about the things that we go through in life because, without God, we would not make it. Some things that we take personal can be understandable, but when it comes to little things that people might say to you out the way when they do not mean any harm by it should not be taking to heart all the time. It is just like being in a relationship, there are some things that your partner may say or do to you that they do not mean any harm or disrespect. I admit that I have took things too seriously in a relationship, but I also learned not to be so serious all the time.

I honestly feel that life is too short to not have some fun occasionally; I mean just acting like you do not have a care in the world and just let yourself be free from responsibilities as an adult especially when going on vacation. We should not let our peace be disturbed by taking things to heart all the time. God expects us to be faithful and honor him in all we do in life and not take things so personal all the time.

One of the main reasons why I was taking things so personal in previous years was because of the things that I had to encounter for little to no reason; for example, when I was in a past

relationship with someone, and they just leave me

abruptly. I was really hurt and confused because it

had me wondering what went wrong. I will admit

that I am an overthinker because of the things that

happened to me in the past however, as I get older,

I had to realize that being an overthinker was doing

me more harm than good because I was always a

guy that was hopping for the best but preparing for

the worst; with that being said, ever since I have

entered adulthood my peace has been in question

because of previous life events that happened to

me from failed potential relationship to just the

people I love either passing away or just going

ghost on me and I honestly believe that it one of the

reasons why I have my guard up all the time.

When I was younger, I had trouble letting things go. I am not saying that I was perfect by any means, but I knew what I brought to the table. Overthinking can hinder you from having and maintaining your peace. We must learn not to take things so seriously all the time for us to have so fun out of life.

In addition to this chapter about not taking things to heart all the time would be don't jump to conclusions. Jumping to conclusions all the time can also hinder your wellbeing as well as your peace. I think that some of the reasons why people jump to conclusions so much is because faith is absent from their lives. God expects us to have faith that things will work out in his time. I also think that the reason some people jump to conclusions so fast because they are so simple-

minded. When being simple-minded all the time, it

can be one of the factors that can stop or cause you

not to have faith that the job that you want God to

do for you to not get done. These are some of the

reasons why we shouldn't take things to heart all

the time; there are many more, but I only talked

about a few. Again, I am no expert on anything that I

talk about in this book, but I do give the best advice

that I can based on my personal experiences.

CHAPTER 4

Express Yourself

People express themselves in many ways; it could

be through sports, singing, or just drawing just to

name a few things. I learn how to personally

express myself through my writing. Writing can be

a haven for some people and to be honest, I think

that is the case for me. Expressing yourself can be

one of many ways to maintain your peace.

One way to express yourself is to talk about your feelings to people. Some people may be afraid to talk about what they are feeling in the heat of the moment because they are either in fear of it costing them a relationship or just scared of what a person may think. We must learn to say what we are feeling to keep our peace in tacked. I recall for a long time that I was one of them people that wouldn't say anything even though I was hurting on the inside because I either thought that people did not care, or they would make me feel even worse than before I started talking about my feelings. I had to learn that talking about your feelings to somebody that cares will help you feel a little better as far as vindication is concerned. We all feel vindicated when we get certain things off or our chest so to speak.

There is not anything wrong with expressing yourself at all. People express themselves in many ways either by writing or just being outspoken about certain topics. Maintaining your peace by expressing yourself is an important thing to do because it can help relieve stress that may been building up for quite some time. Some people are afraid to express themselves just out of fear and the perception of people.

Another way to express yourself is to mean what you say. When you mean what you say about certain situations as far as peace is concerned, you are setting your own boundaries. The words boundaries and express can go hand in hand because when you mean what you say about a certain situation by expressing how you feel about things, you are not any longer a person that is going to agree with certain things that go on in life especially when they are wrong. My mother used to always say to me that *"When you feel like you are right about something, stand on it."* God also expects us to be bonded when it comes to being a follower of him. Do not get me wrong we all fall short of God's glory, but he shows us mercy and pardon each day of our lives.

Meaning what you say is one of the best ways to maintaining and protecting your peace from anyone or anything. You do not have to be mean or cruel when you set certain boundaries for you to keep your personal peace and sanity together. If you do not like what is going on rather at your job or at home, it needs to be addressed. I honestly feel that expressing yourself in a positive way can be a part of the solution instead of the problem.

I personally never been the arguing or fussing type of person however, when things are disturbing my peace then it should not be a problem with me addressing it. I also think that you must stand on what you say by meaning every single word. <u>Malcolm X</u> once said that *"If a man does not stand for something he will fall for everything."* Always learn to stand up for what is right. Life is too short to not have your mind be at peace. Meaning what you say to someone rather it is good or bad can also help you maintain your peace and have a healthier mind in the long run.

Listening more than you speak can help you express yourself even more because people are going to wonder why you are so quiet and observant all the time. Listening before you speak can help you figure out certain things that are going on rather than talking over someone all that time. People often jump to conclusions without listening to either the whole story or just talking over other people when expressing themselves. It is not good to just talk over people and jump to conclusions when you do not know either the whole story or situation.

Trying to understand another person's point of view can be another way to express yourself. Everyone has an opinion and deserves to be heard. When you listen and understand, the outlook on life can be a little bit better. Life is hard enough as it is, but maintaining your peace can be a challenge sometimes especially when you are one of them people that are trying to do the right thing all the time.

One of the best ways to expressing yourself is making eye contact with anyone that you talk to. Some people may look down when talking to people, especially those in high authority. I had trouble making eye contact when I was growing up; but for me to get where I needed to be or wanted to go in life, I had to break that habit. It is just like when we are applying for a job for the first time; when you don't look that person in the eye in an interview then you might not get taken seriously.

Making eye contact with someone is also important when trying to express yourself.

CHAPTER 5

Freeing Your Mind

Keeping your peace is very important, but for that to happen we must learn to free our mind of unnecessary things that may hinder us or be a distraction. When it comes to having peace, it all starts inside our minds. We must have peace of mind within ourselves. Freeing your mind of things that we cannot control is an excellent start to having peace in life.

It is easy for a person who doesn't have a care in the world to say your mind must be free however, it is like that old saying goes; *"unless you have walked a mile in their shoes then you shouldn't judge."* I am guilty of judging people from time to time I mean well all are because we or on the outside looking in, however when some people smile, they do it just to keep the tears from falling. It is important to be at peace with yourself first before taking any kind of action in life.

One way to free your mind of stuff that we may not have any control over is by not worrying so much. Trying to cut down on worrying about unnecessary things can be a challenge especially when you enter adulthood. I recall my mother telling me when I was younger that she would have sleepless nights worrying about how she was going

to pay for this or that for us kids, but then I also

seen her get on her knees and pray about it.

God also tells us not to worry about things in

life. We must trust that God will come through and

get the job done. Our faith sometimes grows weak

from time to time, but when God is involved, all

things are possible. Worrying and stress do go

hand in hand because the more we worry about

thing that we may not have any control over, the

more stressed out we may get. Stress can cause us

to be in a dangerous situation where it may be hard

but not impossible to get out of. We are not always

going to be stress or worry free; we must learn to

try our best to keep the worrying to a minimum and

trust God a lot more. We also find more peace

within ourselves when we worry less. God wants

us to come to him like kids go to their parents for

anything they may need in life. I am not saying that

if you worry less, you will have a stress-free life by

any means; what I am saying is that you will be at

peace within yourself a lot more and your posture

will improve.

Another way to have peace of mind is to talk

things out. Some people much rather yell,

disrespect, or make a fool of themselves just

because they feel superior; the trust be told, we are

all the same in God's eyes. We must learn to talk

things out without being disrespectful to each

other. When you have something that needs to be

addressed, don't hold it on, talk it out. Holding

things in when an issue needs to be addressed can do more harm than good.

When we learn to talk things out, it can free our minds so we can be at peace with ourselves. We must have a clear mind for positive things to happen to us in life. I personally do not like being around people that is always negative and having a simple/closed mind all the time because people like that will destroy your peace of mind if you let them. We must also learn to be a little more optimistic during certain situations in life because sometimes that's all we must keep the peace within ourselves as well as our sanity. I made this personal saying to myself; if it's going to cost me my sanity, then I do not want anything to do with the situation at hand no matter what it is rather it is job, life partner, or people in general. I do not see anything wrong with a little divine intervention because we all need it every now and then.

Meditating can be another way to free your mind of things that you may be currently worrying about. When you meditate, you must learn to lose yourself and be relaxed during the process. It also can be a certain kind of therapy that can be used to get rid of stress that live has to offer. Stress can also be the main thing that can cause us to have a nervous breakdown. I personally do not meditate as often as I should, but that is about to change.

I recall a time when I was in college that when I had my finals coming up that I would sit in my dorm room and meditate for about an hour. I was so nervous for this test that I almost lost faith that I wasn't going to pass because I let distractions come in and take over my mind. A friend of mine gave me some advice about being at peace when it comes to taking quizzes/test. Once I started meditating before each final, the nervous moments started to go away. I also wasn't as worried as I was before meditating. Relaxing your mind before the big moment can help relieve some stress as well as them anxious moment we may have from time to time. Always remember that for our souls to be at peace we must learn not to stress as much.

CHAPTER 6

Letting go of the past can be a challenge sometimes depending on the situation or events that may have transpired during that time. I honestly think we all have a hard time letting things go from time to time because a lot of people live with hurt in their lives either we have lost loved ones or just have so much anger that they may do anything to get revenge on the people that may have wronged us. Revenge is a sucker's game in my opinion because sometimes it may cost you from either getting blessings from God or your life. The best revenge is none because it is like what it says in the bible you reap what you sow. Just because you get forgiveness from God doesn't mean you will get away with it. God wants us to live each day happy, but if we do not learn to let go of the past then we will not be at peace with him at all. Making peace with God is the most important thing to do because when you do his will and obey the gospel, you will have everlasting life.

When moving on from the past, you must identify what is keeping you from going forward. We cannot move on or go forward if we keep looking back; I personally had to learn that when I realized that my past relationship was over. It took almost

two years to move on because I was still in love

with her; it also took people to tell me to move on

from her because my mind wasn't at peace, and it

would have hindered me from getting into another

relationship. Sometimes when you try to find the

source of the issue that keeps us from moving on

can be hard.

Fear can be one of the main factors that can

stop us from either being at peace or just moving

forward in life. Life is too short to be dwelling in the

past and wishing it would have been different. We

must move on to bigger and better things for us to

be a success in what we may be trying to

accomplish in life. Fear can also stop us from

taking some risk to better ourselves, but for that to

happen we must learn how to face our fears when

it comes to keeping the peace and maintaining it.

Identifying what is keeping us from moving forward

is a start in the right direction. We must be honest

with ourselves for us to move forward and quit

looking back because what is done is done.

Having difficulty with letting go of the past will likely be related to one of the following key emotions.

- *Guilt*

- *Regret*

- *Sadness*

- *Anger*

Guilt will be the first emotions that I will be talking about. For example, you may be feeling guilty for not spending enough time with your parents or just being disrespectful to them, but when they pass away you may be starting to think that maybe you should have spent more time or just respected them a lot better than you did. Your mind is not at peace at all because you all a sudden have regret. The point of this example is that we need to think things through before acting. Life is too short to live with the guilt that we may have in the past. It is best to move on with our lives and put the past behind us for us to move on and have the peace that we need to go forward in life. It is hard to move on when you are one of those people who lost both of your parents; that is why we must pray each day that God will get us through things.

The second thing that can keep us moving on or letting the past stay where it's at would be the word regret. We all regret some things that we may have said or done in the past however, there are consequences in what we do or say rather good or bad. Some people live with more regret than others.

Sadness can be a huge factor that can keep us from moving on from the past. You may be feeling a certain type of way when it comes to moving on however, we often make it hard on ourselves. I really believe it is a process that we must go through in life because sadness can be

an emotion that can keep us from having a

peaceful mind; it can also distract us from

accomplishing certain goals that we may want to

achieve one day. Sadness can come from

anything rather it be a lost loved one or just

having a bad day just to name a few examples.

We do have a choice; either try to find things that

will keep us at a peaceful state or just let

yourself go into a dark place in your mind where

it can be a challenge to get out.

The word anger can keep you from letting go

of the past because when it is constantly on your

mind, you are not at peace with yourself. The

words regret and anger can go hand in hand

when it comes to letting go of the past. It is like

what was stated before what is done is done; we cannot get yesterday back. You may get angry at your job or something, however you don't address the issue right then and there, so now you may have regret because you didn't say anything. I have honestly seen that happen a bunch of times and their peace of mind wasn't right because they have so much regret that it is making them angry on the inside. We should not let anger destroy or dictate how we act or treat people.

The last thing that I will be talking about when it comes to letting go of the past is grudge holding. Let's face it, everyone has held a grudge against someone or something before; holding grudges can hinder us from getting the blessings from God. Grudge holding can also be exhausting because when you talk and think about it all the time not only your mind is not at peace you also cannot move on. When you go up to someone and talk about the same situation over and over, the person that you may be confiding to will sooner or later get tired of listening to the same negativity.

SOME KEY THINGS TO DO AND REALIZE WHEN HOLDING ON TO AN OLD GRUDGE

1. *Deal with the realization that the other party will not apologize for what they may have done to you.*

2. *Forgive them and move on and try to keep a peaceful mindset.*

3. *Practice empathy.*

4. *Start writing a journal.*

CHAPTER 7

Never hold your feelings in for too long

Sometimes, holding your feelings in for too long can do more harm than good. What needs to be said or addressed needs to be; it is just like being in a relationship, when one party does not express his or her feelings then the misunderstanding of things starts to happen. We all have a tough time saying what we feel from time to time.

When you and another party have a clear understanding about what is going on, then things will be less confusing and complicated. You will be at peace a lot more when expressing your feelings to someone because it is like a huge burden that has be lifted off your shoulders. Keeping your feelings on mute all the time can mess with your mind and peace at the same time.

There are many ways to express how you may be feeling in that moment. Some people may take longer than others to tell a person how they may be feeling because they are either too shy or just afraid of what people may think about them. Never be afraid of what people may think about you because at the end of the day them same people do not pay your bills nor put a roof over your head.

Holding your feeling in for too long can mess with you in a phycological way.

I have personally seen people lose themselves just because they were afraid to express their feelings. I had trouble saying and expressing how I felt during certain situations because of the fear of being belittled or called weak. Do not ever think that it is weak to say or express the way that you are feeling in certain situations especially when being a man.

Some people may think that men are not supposed to show emotion or cry; people forget that men have feelings to as well as being human. I honestly think that men need emotional support like women be getting it because again men are human to and how they feel matters as well. Men deserve to be happy like women do; it is a two-way streak. I also believe that one of the reasons that the suicide rate is higher for men than women is because they feel like he doesn't have anyone to talk to about their feelings especially when they feel like their girlfriend or wife will use it against them or it could be just the fear of being belittled or talked about negatively. I do not know about some people, but I will personally say and express what I may be feeling doing certain situations even if it cost me my relationship; that was a decision that I made a long time ago after I got out of a toxic relationship years ago with my ex.

Saying What You Feel

Some people may mistake saying what you feel is disrespectful however, I honestly think that it will give you peace of mind. Some things we need

to say need to be out in the open. You do not have to

be mean when saying what you feel; some people's

tone of voice may change when doing so as well as

their vocabulary. Choose your world wisely. We

must learn to get things off our chest because

when dealing with people in the world, we must be

straight to the point and not beating around the

bush so to speak. We shouldn't feel bad about

saying what we feel either. Some people do not

have any problem with being outspoken, so that is

how they can express themselves and get their

point across. Just because you say what you feel

does not mean that you are right all the time either.

If you feel like you may be right about something,

then stand on it and do not back down.

Maintaining Your Sanity

There are many ways to maintain your sanity. The way that the word insanity is defined would be repeating the same behavior and expecting a different outcome. The words sanity and peace go hand in hand because sometimes if you don't have peace in your life, you can lose your sanity.

Key things to do when trying to maintain your

sanity

1. Try to focus on the positives.

2. Take it a day at a time.

3. Do not worry too much about the future.

4. Do not stress over things you cannot control.

CHAPTER 8

Making Some Important Changes to Your Life

When making important changes to your life, your mind must be at peace because distractions can come from anywhere. We must learn to deal with the fact that for us to make the necessary changes in our lives, we must do things that we do not want to do. Distractions can stop us from doing a lot of positive things that can help us make them important changes.

When you have that peaceful mindset, all the other things that may come into your life will not be so overwhelming. Life can be a challenge sometimes because of our mindset we may have the fear of failing or just being simple-minded which means that we are not caring or willing to learn something new. We learn something new every day whether it is good or bad. God wants us to be at peace with others as well as ourselves.

Some people may be afraid of change because of the simple reason of not wanting to adapt and thrive. I was afraid of change because of my mindset at the time when I was younger however, I had to learn from my mother when she told me that change is part of life. We will all have

to go through change no matter what it is because

it is inevitable. Sometimes, changing our lives for

the better comes with sacrifices; it can be from

losing friends to just cutting back on the things that

we may love or do.

Following God and obeying the gospel comes

with sacrifices. When it comes to dedicating your

life to God and obey him, sacrifices must be made.

We cannot just say that we believe in God and not

obey and do his will; Jesus said this in the bible,

"Not everyone who says to Me, Lord Lord, shall

enter the kingdom of heaven, but he who does the

will of My Father in heaven. Many will say to Me in

that day, Lord Lord, have we not prophesied in your

name, cast out demons in your name, and done

many wonders in your name? And I will declare to them, I never knew you; depart from Me, you who practice lawlessness!" (Matthew 7: 21-23)

In life we must learn to let things go whether it's an old relationship or old job. Moving on may be hard sometimes however, for us to make positive changes in our lives, certain things must be done to make it happen. When we move on from things that are hindering us from either being at peace or making positive changes, we become better people and able to handle the challenges that life has to offer accordingly.

CHAPTER 9

Thinking Positive

Thinking positively is one of the most important things to do when maintaining and protecting your peace. You never want to be around or be a person who is so negative all the time because it can destroy your positive mindset. People who are always negative all the time are wondering why good things do not happen to them; the reason why is that they do not look at the positive things that may be going on now. God

wants us to stay positive, but he also knows that

we are human, and we fall short of his glory daily.

I am not saying that when you think positive

good things are going to happen all the time

however, you will have a better peace of mind when

you do. We must learn to be more optimistic about

certain things and not jump to conclusions all the

time during certain situations; we are all guilty of

that from time to time. We must stay positive for us

to keep our peace with others as well as ourselves.

Three best ways to think Positive during certain

Situations in Life

1. Block out negative thoughts

2. Get rid of negative people.

3. Smile a little bit more.

BLOCKING OUT NEGATIVE THOUGHTS

Blocking out negative thoughts can be hard especially if you are an overthinker. Some people have that mentality that hopping for the best and preparing for the worst; I mean it is a good thing to have, but we also must learn to trust God a lot more than we have been to get the job done for us.

Our minds be a peace a lot more when we learn to minimize our negative thoughts. Do not be so judgmental or so quick to jump to conclusions all the time when life is not either going your way or feeling like all is lost. God can come out of anywhere and make things better for us in his time; he is always on time with everything. Life is too short to be having negative thoughts all the time during certain situations especially when things start to get a little hard. Even when we follow God and do his good will we are going to have our stumbling blocks in front of us that we must get over and go past. God will give you peace and rest if you have faith that he will get the job done.

GETTING RID OF NEGATIVE PEOPLE

Trying to get rid of people that is negative all the time sounds easy however, it is a lot harder than what you may think. Negative people can be your so-called associates that may not have your best interest at heart or just fake friends that try to throw shade on what you may be trying to accomplish in life. for some people it is easy to get rid of negative people, but for others it can be a challenge because of either their perception of you or worried about what they may think. Sometimes you cannot change the perception of people. When it involves keeping your peace of mind you must do what is necessary to maintain it.

Ways of get rid of negative people in your life

- Create time for yourself.
- Leave a conversation when a person is negative all the time.

SMILE A LITTLE BIT MORE

Smiling a lot more can help you think positively and be more at peace with yourself. I remember that my mother always kept a smile on her face because she was always thinking positive, especial in tough situations. In life, we often see that some people would be miserable no matter what you do for them or what you say that is positive. It is important to be optimistic when it comes to certain situations.

Some people who are always miserable cannot stand when another person is always smiling all the time. I personally hate being around somebody that is so negative that you hate to see them coming or just listening to them talk about a certain situation so bad that they feel like there is not any light at the end of the tunnel so to speak. Smiling is not only healthy for us, but it also helps us to have and maintain peace of mind positively.

CHAPTER 10

Love Yourself

Always remember before you can love someone else, you must learn to love yourself first and foremost. My honest opinion on how to love yourself would be knowing what your purpose is in life; some people do not understand what their purpose is because they be so busy trying to worry about what people may think of them. It may take certain people a long time to come to the realization that people do not want to see you

happy in your own skin metaphorically speaking of

course.

When we start to love ourselves and learn to

be comfortable in our skin, then we will start to

care less of what people may think of us and finally

have some peace of mind. God wants us to love

ourselves as well as be happy and humble when it

comes to him because no matter what happens in

life God is always in control. I honestly think that

loving yourself is one of the most important things

to do especially when you may feel like all is lost or

there is not any hope for you. Faith in God that he

will get the job done is all you need.

One of the most critical things that we must

learn when it comes to loving ourselves is knowing

our worth. Knowing your worth will have you at peace with yourself. It takes some people a very long time to know their worth because for one reason they are trying to please others for validation. Some people lose themselves because they may either be trying too hard to keep others happy while being miserable themselves or just putting themselves last. Never lose yourself or your peace of mind when dealing with people who are not any good; it is unhealthy and can cause you to lose your sanity.

I personally made up my mind a long time ago by refusing to keep someone that is ungrateful toward me happy all the time when I am miserable in the process especially when it comes to relationships. Knowing your worth is important when it comes to relationships whether you are

and man or a woman. Life is too short to be

miserable with someone that is ungrateful toward

you. A man's happiness matters as well as a

woman's do. God gives us all the warning signs

when it comes to leaving a bad relationship

however, we still may hold onto the little glimmer

of hope that things are going to get better. It is just

like a woman that may be going through an abusive

relationship and does not have the courage to

leave; there may be many factors on why people do

not leave bad relationships either because their

self-esteem is so low that they feel like they cannot

get anyone else or just hanging on to that person

for financial reasons just to name a few.

When you know that you have either been a good man or woman and the relationship ends, you are going to be sad at first when the breakup is still fresh however, as time goes on your mind will be at peace. Never be a prisoner of your own past because you truly cannot move on when your mind is not at peace. We must be at peace within ourselves when trying to move on from a person.

In addition to loving yourself, we must learn that it is ok to make mistakes. When making mistakes it is important to learn from them, so we do not repeat them. You learn better you do better. Some people will judge you when making mistakes however, it is your responsibility to either learn from them or fall into that trap by worrying about what people may think or say about you.

Putting yourself first can be one of the things to do when trying to love yourself. Setting boundaries for yourself means that your care about your wellbeing as well as your worth. When putting yourself first, it is not that you are trying to be selfish; it is more so that you do not have to tolerate disrespect, your boundaries being breached, or your peace disturbed. We must learn how to do what is best for ourselves in life regardless of what people may think about us. Everyone will not agree with what you may say or do all the time; that is why it is important to love yourself before loving anyone else.

Another way to learn how to love yourself is learning to see the beauty in the simple things in life. We must learn to be thankful for the simple things in life because some people never get the

chance to enjoy them. Making your passion a

priority is one of the important things to do when

loving yourself. Regardless of what people may

think or how hard it gets, go after the goals that

you want to accomplish one day. Believe it or not

some people do not want to see you secede in life

when it comes to being passionate about what you

want to do in life; avoiding people like that and

setting boundaries will help you not only to love

yourself more but to find and maintain the peace in

life that you may been looking for a long time. I

know that I said something about not being selfish

however, sometimes you must be when it comes to

either your peace or loving yourself all over again.

CHAPTER 11

Connect with the People you Love and Trust

When your mind is at peace you can start to

connect with people that you love and trust. For us

to love someone there must be some trust

established first. Without trust, there is no love.

Some people may have very few or zero people

that they trust, however, to be honest when you do

not trust anyone it can create some problems in the

future. Also, when you do not trust anybody, the disappointment will not bother you as much.

Some people are so used to disappointment that they may anticipate it coming from a mile away. It is always important to have an open mind about people as well as things that may be going on. Trust is an organic thing that should be earned over time. It is just like being in a relationship; both parties that are involved must trust before they love each other. I see relationships in this generation come to an end because either social media or just letting other people get in their ear with negativity. You and your partner may be asking each other where was the peace and love that we had for one another. When it comes to trusting your partner in the relationship, there are some things that both parties should talk about so there is a clear

understanding of what is going on so no one will

get hurt.

Sometimes, it is better for a person to have a

few selections of friends. The smaller your circle

the better off you are because the last thing that

you may want to deal with is chaos. We must have

trust in someone for them to be our friend.

One of the things to do when it comes to

connecting with people is to make eye contact. Eye

contact can be a tough thing to do sometimes

however, for a person to take you seriously, you

must learn to look them straight in the eye. It is not

about intimidation; it is about being serious about

what you want and your intentions. When you look

down or away from a person that may be talking to

you, they are not either going to take you seriously or think that you may have a hidden agenda that may not be good. I had a hard time looking a person in the eye when I was younger, when I got older, I realized how important it was.

Also, when you encounter people that you love and trust you are at peace most of the time. One major thing that needs to be done is to schedule some quality time. When scheduling time with people make sure that they are either not busy or in a bad mood, because them two things can ruin the peace and vibe by giving off negative energy.

CHAPTER 12

Talking and Praying to God a lot More

When it comes to protecting your peace, letting God be involved is a must. At the end of the day, God is in control of everything. Talking to God each day when going through good or bad times is a must as well; he is a just God who forgives and provides. When talking to God, our minds will start to be at peace. I honestly believe that is it important for us to make our peace and have a relationship with God that no man can break; for that to happen we must get to know him first.

God knows that we are not perfect however, he expects us to believe, have faith, a do his will according to the bible. It is an amazing feeling when you have peace with God because your faith gets stronger as well as your belief in him. Following, obeying, and praising God are the most important things to do for us to have peace in our lives. I am not saying that everything is going to be easy because when doing the right thing, we must learn to make some unpopular decisions that our peers may not agree with.

One way to find peace with God is to praise him more. Times will become a challenge, but the people who make it through them are the real

winners. Tough times do not last forever. Even

when you may feel like that all is lost and feeling

discouraged you must praise God. God is good all

the time, and if we keep our faith anything is

possible. Praise God in the good and bad times.

Reading the bible can also allow us to have

peace and a better relationship with God. The more

we read the bible the better we get to know God.

The Bible is unlike any other book because almost

every word has a meaning behind it; it is also called

the sword of the spirit. The Bible can also teach us

about peace and how to maintain it. When finding

peace in life, we must make sure that we maintain

it and do not let anyone, or anything destroy it. I am

not saying that finding peace by reading the bible

will solve your problem however, you will have a

clear perspective on what it takes to follow God

and keep the peace. God wants us to be at peace

with not only ourselves but with other people in

general.

Finally, when you have the desire for solitude,

take your time and go on walks by yourself. When

you feel comfortable with your solitude, all you care

about is peace; the smaller your circle of friends

the less drama you must deal with. Some people

find solace when being alone, especially for a long

period. Solace and peace go hand in hand because

peace is when nothing bothers you and the word

solace means that you have finally found relief

after you may have gone through hardship. When

you get closer to God, you will find solace and

peace.

CHAPTER 13

Listen to your Inner Voice

Listening to your inner voice can get you into

some good and bad situations. When you feel like

something is not right or too good to be true, then

most or the time it is. Maintaining your peace has a

lot to do with following your gut feeling so to speak.

It is not always good or smart to be and follower all

the time. Even when becoming a Christian for the

first time the temptation comes after you twice as

hard as before. Over time, when we become stronger in our faith in God, we will be able to resist temptation better.

Paying attention to our surroundings when it comes to keeping the peace is one of the most important things to do. Do not be so quick to jump to conclusions on certain situations without thinking things through. Paying attention does pay dividends in the long run. We also miss out on certain things when we do not listen to our inner voice however, it can also be a blessing in disguise. Sometimes, paying attention to your gut feeling is a good quality to have because when you feel that something is not right or something is about to transpire in a bad way, your gut feeling comes into play.

Protecting Your Peace by Any Means Necessary

There are many ways to listen to your inner voice. Maintaining your peace also has a lot to do with your inner voice. God has given us five senses for a reason. We all want peace in our lives however, when you just react to emotions without thinking things through the consequences can be catastrophic. Some people do not think before they react.

Pause and breathe can be another way to listen to your inner voice. We must learn to take a deep breath and think about things before making any moves in life. Pausing can also help you communicate with your inner voice because sometimes when you pause and think about what you are trying to do it can help in the long run.

CHAPTER 14

Test your Limits

Testing your limits can be a challenge when it comes to keeping your peace. However, it is like that old saying goes only the strong survive. When life is filled with hardship, those who are the survivors try to turn something negative into something positive. When trying to make the best out of a bad situation, we must learn to have that inner peace with ourselves. I personally refuse to be around people that always either jump to

conclusions or just act like all is lost before going

into battle so to speak. I honestly would do my best

to stay away from people like that because I

personally feel like my peace is being disturbed.

Never let anyone take your joy or hinder you from

being successful in life. Always have that positive

mindset that there is always a way out of a bad

situation; also have faith in God that he will get the

job done.

God is going to test our limits from time to

time. It is up to us to be up for the challenge. God

also expects us to be faithful and trust in him even

in challenging times; even some of the greats in the

bible have been tested by God so they can do his

will. The Lord wants us to be happy with it comes to both serving him and being at peace.

When keeping your peace intact, your limits are going to be tested. I really think that our anger and patience are tested daily especially when working at a nine to five job. I am sure there are plenty of times that people wanted to walk out on a job, however when you have a family to support you must take the good with the bad sometimes. I personally have had days when I would wonder if it was going to be my last working at this job.

It is always good to have patience when it comes to keeping the peace however, the word patience can only go so far. God also tells us to not be so quick to anger all the time. Emotions can be a little bit tricky to control rather you are in a relationship or just doing a project with someone

that you may not be getting along with. It is as is

said before it is sometimes better to be at peace

than it is to be right. When you know in your heart

that you are right about something, why waste time

trying to convince a person that is either stubborn

or does not want to listen to you? Some people's

way of keeping the peace is by not saying anything

at all because of the fear of an argument and loss

of a relationship.

There is a lot of give and take when it comes

to being in a relationship. Men are more logical

than women are because women react to what they

are feeling in the heat of the moment while men

think about the logic behind the current situation; I

honestly think that is why arguments occur. Men

and women both need each other; that is why God said that the man is head of the household as well as the provider and the woman takes care of the inside of the house as well as nurture and brings the children up the right way in the eyes of the lord. Your limits will be tested when it comes to keeping a successful marriage together.

Another thing when it comes to testing your limits is visualizing success. When it comes to the word success, sacrifices must be made as well. Sacrifices can be from missing out on temporary fun to keeping a budget on what you may be spending your money on. Our peace will also be tested when it comes to trying to accomplish certain goals in life. Protecting your peace first and foremost when it comes to your goals is a must.

Visualizing success means in most people's own words, trying to imagine that what you may want to acquire or achieve is already there; you just must do the hard work to make it a reality. God will also push you to the limit to make things happen in his time. Everything that we ask for from God happens in his time, not ours. What is meant for you will happen. Our peace should be a top priority when it comes to testing our limits; we must also be clearheaded.

You may have heard the old saying that hanging on to someone or something is a lot more painful than just letting go; letting go can be a challenge depending on the situation. Always choose peace of chaos because at the end of the day being at peace can save you a lot of grief. It is just like I said before you can be the one that seeks

peace and be a part of the chaos/problem at the

same time.

CHAPTER 15

Being Kind to People

When it comes to maintaining our peace, we must learn to do our part in the process. You can either be a part of the problem or a solution. One of the things that we must do when it comes to keeping the peace is to be kind to one another; for some people that can be a tall order. My mother always used to tell me that you owe anybody the time of day. Sometimes, even just speaking to a person can make their day a lot better because you may not know what kind of mental battles they may be struggling with.

Some people much rather not speak to you when it comes to an issue that they may have. I think that it would be best to clear the air and talk about what is going on and how it can be rectified. Some issues can be fixed if we just learn to talk about it and maybe come up with a positive solution to the problem at hand. We all have let pride get in the way rather it comes to relationships, friendship, or even a perfect stranger. Our pride can also cost us in the end if peace is not established again.

We as humans do not like to admit when we are wrong during some situations; that is when we need to put our pride aside and try to fix whatever is going on. You do not have to be loud or use profanity to get your point across because that does nothing but eliminate the possibility for peace.

I personally never liked to be mean to people for no reason, however, we are human and in the heat of the moment we may say things that we do not mean and regret it in the long run. Be careful with what you say because it might turn around on you. Some people want peace however, they are the cause of the chaos and drama; they are the people that we must learn to stay away from because their bad influences can rub off in a bad way.

CHAPTER 16

Facing Your Fears

Facing your fears can be a challenge especially when it comes to protecting your peace. I feel that we must learn to be brave and set boundaries when it comes to keeping the peace. One of the reasons that some people stay in the same rut is that they may either be afraid to fail or just worried about what their peers may think.

When it comes to facing our fears, we must learn to accept the outcome. It can be hard saying what you feel because of the fear of negative backlash; for us to maintain our peace, we must conquer the fears that we may have that are hindering us from either being at peace with ourselves or leveling up in life in a positive way. Fear can stop a lot of things in either a positive or negative way. Never be afraid to do or say things that will help keep the peace.

WAYS TO FACE OUR FEARS

1. Talk about it.

2. Don't try to be perfect.

3. Visualize a happy place.

Talk about it

Talking about your fears with someone else can be a challenge within its right however, one of the best ways to be at peace is by letting it out to someone that you can trust. You may have heard that old saying, "Do not trust anybody"; there is some truth to that statement however, we must learn to trust someone in this world otherwise we will be all alone. It may take some people a longer time to talk about their fears than others because some people just do not like sharing their thoughts or feelings.

I honestly felt that on a personal level, the only one that I could talk to about what was bothering me was my mother. It is not good to talk about your fears to everyone; only have a select few that you can trust to have them long/deep conversations with. After having that much-needed

conversation, you will feel a lot better that you got

what was bothering you off your chest and you feel

more at peace.

Don't try to be Perfect

It is ok to be afraid of certain things; we are

not perfect, and God knows that. God does expect

us to do the best we can in everything positive that

we do in life. God knows we fall short of his glory

daily, but when we do our best to serve him, good

things start to happen and the hard times that we

had to go through start to pay off. Always keep your

faith that God will get the job done.

Visualize a Happy Place

We can manifest a lot of things, but when it

comes to keeping and maintaining your peace, that

by itself can be a challenge within its right.

Everyone wants to be happy, successful, and

worry-free however, that does not happen for

everyone for several reasons because certain

people may either be the cause of the chaos or just

have that simple mindset that everything is always

negative coming out of their mouth. When we start

to learn how to be more optimistic about life in

general, things will start to get better. We must

learn that for us to have peace in our lives it must

start with a positive mindset and learn how to face

our fears. We must learn to do this when it comes

to maintaining peace and fear can destroy our

minds if we let it.

CHAPTER 17

Being Grateful for What We Have

It is important to be grateful for what we have because some people may be in worse situations than we are. God can give, but he can also take away. Always remain humble no matter what because life is too short to not either be at peace or have selfish ways. I will be the first one to admit that I have laughed at people for being less fortunate when I was young however, as I have gotten older, I started to think before I acted

because God could have put me in that same

unfortunate situation.

I do not know about anyone else, but I like my

mind and well-being to be at peace instead of being

unhappy or anxious all the time. Being at peace

with certain things is not a sign that you are weak;

some people much rather have a sane mind

without all the drama than being a person who is

either always in someone else's business or

causing malice/chaos. Some people thrive on

drama because they either do not have a life or

they are envy of what other people may have.

When trying to maintain our peace, we must

learn not to complain about the things we do not

have. Maybe it is not our time for certain things to

happen yet because, at the end of the day, God has

the final say so and is in control of every situation.

God may be keeping us out of trouble when he

doesn't bless us with what we may want right away.

I am personally thankful for what I have because it

is like I said before some people have worse

situations to deal with than we do. Always give God

the praise no matter what even in the challenging

times.

It is also important that when people are

starting to have things go their way always

remember to be happy for them because your time

is coming. I recall times that I would be sad and

lonely because it has been so long since I have

been in a relationship however, I remained

steadfast and kept my faith in God that he would

send me someone who is not only good for me but has a kind and peaceful heart. I will also admit that I was told that I would never get in a relationship because I was too nice; the people that told me that were trying to destroy my peace and I had to just stay away from people like that because sometimes in life they do not want to see you doing better than them. In my heart, I knew my time was coming and it came; I am thankful that I have the patience to wait on God to send me someone good for me and likewise good for her. God does hear our prayers and I trust and believe in him every day of my life.

CHAPTER 18

Avoid Self-Pity

There are many ways to keep the peace; what I will be talking about in this chapter is how to avoid self-pity. Self-pity can come from anything. How it is defined would be excessive, self-absorbed unhappiness over one's own troubles; trying to avoid self-pity can be a hard thing to do sometimes. It can also hinder our minds from being at peace with ourselves. We are all human and make mistakes from time to time however, it is not ok to make the same ones repeatedly.

It is also not good to be self-absorbed because the perception of that would be that people will think that you are all about yourself. Coming off as being selfish is not good because people will not want to have anything to do with you because, for one reason, they feel like their peace is disturbed. I was always told that if you are on your feet help the next person that may need it.

Self-pity can also come from not wanting to help other people out and you start to feel some type of way when things start to happen to that person that you denied negatively. The older we get the more we have a clear understanding of why it is important to be at peace with ourselves as well as others.

Another way to avoid self-pity would be telling the truth and not feeling bad about it afterward. I respect a person a lot better when they tell me the truth about myself because it helps me to be at peace with certain things as well as becoming a better person. The truth will set you free. I have also learned that when you constantly tell lies that you must tell them back-to-back to cover up the lie you just told. You are not just creating chaos; you are building a mental prison in your mind. Some people have told lies for so long that over time they start to believe them and that is a dangerous trait to have.

Life is too short to have been feeling bad for telling the truth because at the end of the day God is going the judge us for the works that we have done, and we also will have to answer for the times that we did not ask for forgiveness. Always tell the truth to either your friend, partner, or just anyone that you may meet because at the end of the day the truth will me you free from the prison of your own mind.

In addition, when avoiding self-pity, we must stay away from people that like to gaslight others. The definition of the word gaslight is the practice of psychologically manipulating someone into questioning their own sanity, memory, or powers of reasoning. A person that gaslights others all the time can be very cunning and deceitful. I personally had to deal with an ex-girlfriend years ago who had mom and dad issues; I had to decide that I was not going to deal with her anymore for me to maintain my peace and be happy.

A very manipulative person will gaslight you till there is no end in sight if you let them however, when your mind is at peace with everything around you then you should not be bothered. NEVER let a person have mental power over your thoughts or peace. We all must learn to let people get on down the road that lie or gaslight all the time until there is no end.

Never fell bad or have self-pity when it comes to setting boundaries to maintain your peace.

CHAPTER 19

The Smaller your Inner Circle the Better

When dealing with a select few people, less

drama and chaos can be avoided. Some people like

their solitude so much that they will do anything to

protect their peace. It is not that they feel like they

are better than the next person; it is that they will

pick peace over drama any day of the week. Only

the people who keep it real and straight up from

the start have very few friends because some people much rather do or say what is popular than what is right.

The people who stay to themselves all the time tend to have more boundaries because their peace of mind and sanity are at stake. I personally never want to lose my sanity over something that is either irrelevant or stupid; that is why I am one of those people who like my solitude a lot. Being at peace is important because you will have a better outlook on life in general.

Having a small circle of friends means that you trust very few people. Some people have trust issues because they either have been hurt before or just have that issue of just overthinking. Trust is earned not given. When you violate or take advantage of that trust, it is hard to get it back. It is just like being in a relationship; when your partner cheats on you with someone else, you not only feel betrayed, but you also feel that the trust is gone to the point of no return. Always be careful with who you trust in life because people these days are either all for themselves or playing for keeps.

If a person cannot trust you then how can it be peace between you and the other party? The words trust and peace go hand in hand because when you trust someone with anything rather it is a secret or your life then you can maintain your peace and your mind is at ease. I am not saying that having a lot of friends is a bad thing, but just be selective with who you let in your circle.

One other thing that we must learn when it comes to protecting your peace is to keep certain people out of your business. The more people that know your business the more drama that you must deal with. I am going to use a relationship for example, you never want many people to know what goes on in your personal life because they are either jealous or just cannot wait for the breakup. It is some people who want to not see you happy or at peace with someone including family. We must do what is necessary to protect our peace even if it means losing either a few friends or cutting people off that love to be the cause of the chaos.

CHAPTER 20

Get Some Rest

Our minds need to be at peace before we go to sleep at night. It may take some people longer to fall asleep because they may be so worried that their minds are racing all night long. We all have sleepless nights that we cannot take easy and relax our bodies. However, it all starts with the brain when it comes to getting the required rest we need.

Sometimes, I wish that I did not have a worry or care in the world like a child. It is just like the bible says, *"When I was a child I thought like a child, but when I became a man, I put away my childish games."* We all must grow up sometime otherwise we may never learn about the full potential that life has to offer. We begin to learn right from wrong from infancy to adulthood. We must learn to rest our body otherwise it will shut down and become problematic; that is one of the issues that we do not need when having a sound and peaceful mind.

We also need to learn when to get some rest and it doesn't necessarily have to do with getting more sleep; sleep is essential when it comes to maintaining your peace. The older you get the more we tend to appreciate the small things and look forward to them. Most people look forward to getting to their beds at night because of either a long day or just trying to unwind and have me-time. We all need some of that time now and then even if you are in a relationship, you may want our personal space.

No matter what, always make time for yourself to get some rest. Getting that much-needed me-time can be a challenge for a lot of reasons from making sure the kids are taken care of to just people always asking for favors. I personally like my solitude but when you have kids and responsibilities to take care of as an adult, we tend to let our me-time or personal space fall by the wayside. We must learn to maintain a work-life balance because the body can only take and do so much. Staying up too late can be a bad thing if it is done consistently all the time. Get some rest and do not go to bed mad or upset so your mind is not racing and wandering all night long. Our body will tell us that we need rest and to just take it easy.

I personally do not know a person's situation but as for me it will get some rest and relax my mind and not worry as much. It also says in the bible that when we have faith in God and do his will, he will give us rest and his yoke is easy, and his burden is light. God will take care of all of us and never leave us.

Some people find solace when just looking at a body of water. People find solace in anything; when they find it, it gives some peace of mind depending on what they are doing. Remember, do

not go to bed mad because life is short, and you

never know when God may call you home.

THATS WHAT IT'S ALL ABOUT

CHAPTER 21

Keep a Journal

Keeping a journal can be one of many ways to cope with life in general. You can write about anything from just telling how your day was to just talking about whatever comes to mind. Some people find peace and solace when trying to keep a journal; some people may think by doing so can get what they want to say out.

People express themselves in many ways.

Keeping the peace when keeping a journal can be a

good thing to do. Some people document everything

that they do in life so years later someone could

read it. some people find more peace when writing

than just doing stuff to get enjoyment out of it.

some people cannot wait to write in their journals

during their free time. Writing can be the therapy

that you may be looking for when it comes to

protecting your peace. Some people have a passion

for writing and turn it into a career. Some even

started with journal entries to perfect their craft by

taking their skills to the next level however for that

to happen we must learn to have peace of mind

during the entire process. Some things may be a

challenge to achieve but hard work, persistence,

and dedication will soon pay off especially when God is included during the process.

You cannot keep a good journal if your peace is not maintained in my opinion because if you are trying to work in a place where it is chaotic, the result will not be very good. It is just like working in a place where there is always noise; you will not be able to concentrate or think about what topic you may want to explore. Always do your best to make sure to work in a quiet and peaceful place.

One way to learn how to keep a journal is to write down the things you may have done that day. I honestly think that writing down and taking notes daily can not only improve your writing skills, but it can also give you peace of mind. No one must know what you may be writing about and to be honest I think that it is a good thing for your journal to

remain confidential until the time is right. The more

confidential you are about certain things in life, the

more peace you will find within yourself. You have

them people who cannot wait to get home from

either school or work to just start writing in their

journals because for some of them, it is their way

to escape reality for a few hours. Sometimes we

need that escape from reality even if it is just for a

few minutes. Being in a quiet place is also a way to

find solace in writing a journal.

In addition to writing a journal, some people

use it to write letters to either themselves or

others. I have seen people write to a loved one that

is deceased because that may be their way of

coping with life. Life is hard enough as it is, and

some people may not want to just sit down and

listen to you about what is bothering you. Everyone

needs a shoulder to cry on now and then. Again,

writing and keeping a journal can be a person's way

of dealing with the hardships of life in general.

People feel at peace when it is just them and a

notebook that they can write their deep personal

thoughts in.

Writing down the things that may bother us

can be a stress reliever when it comes to

protecting your peace. Again, some people do not

care about what you may be going through; that is

one of many reasons why some people keep

journals. When you let things out that may be

bothering you emotionally, you may start to feel a

lot better because your mind starts to be at peace

again. There are many ways to protect your peace and I honestly think that keeping a journal and writing things down that you may want to say or do is one of the best ways to do it. Do not let things fester in you for too long because your mind will eventually go crazy.

CHAPTER 22

Create a Positive Morning Routine

Some people may have a different routine when getting up in the morning. When you learn to create and have that positive routine in the morning time, the chances of your day being more productive go up. It is just like waking your child up for school for example, some days they may get up before you do or do not feel like getting up at all.

Also, when creating that morning routine, make sure that you are in a good mood because the tone will be set for the rest of that day. Do not ever go to bed upset because your mind cannot relax and the more you mind is racing at night the less sleep you will get. Always be in good spirits that everything is going to be alright because being optimistic about certain can also help you handle the situation a lot better rather it is a good or bad one.

Some people may find peace in starting their day off with a workout. Working out can be another thing to find solace in and protect your peace. You can also be so caught up in your work that you may feel like you are escaping reality for a few minutes or an hour. I personal like starting my day with either going for a jog or working out because it increases my posture and makes me feel confident that everything it going to be alright; that is how I find my escape.

Another way to keep the peace is to start the morning praying to God. This is something that we all should do first before we do anything else. Praising God in the good and bad times is important; he also wants us to come to him like children go to their parents when they need something. We are all human and fall short of God's glory every day; God also gives us mercy and pardon. Praying to God as part of our routine will help set the tone for that day. You also find peace when talking to God daily. God is and should be everyone's number one priority every day from when we get up in the morning to when we go to

bed at night.

Telling yourself that it is going to be a good

day will help keep that positive morning routine.

Everyone wants to have a great day every day

however, life does not work that way we are going

to have tough and challenging times that we must

endure to be successful in life. It is important to

have that positive mindset that things are going to

be alright even in the darkest times. God will be

with us always even until the end of the world.

Do not let anyone destroy your peace or take

your joy away. Some people do not want to see you

happy because they are miserable themselves and

try to create malice wherever they go. People thrive

on making another person's life miserable simply

because they may not have a life of their own.

Creating that positive morning routine starts with

your mindset on things. Always thank God for

making sure that you get up in the morning

because some people do not make it to the next

day.

CHAPTER 23

Avoid Distractions

One thing in life to learn early on when it comes to maintaining and protecting your peace is to do your best to avoid distractions. Distractions can come from anyone and anywhere. When we become so distracted that we cannot concentrate on an important goal, then we must learn to eliminate ourselves from the things that may

hinder us from keeping the peace.

It is so easy to get distracted because there

may be a lot of things that could be going on at one

time. We must learn to have peace of mind to

accomplish the goals that we may have. When

someone is wasting your time for example can also

be a distraction. Do not let anyone waste your time

on anything rather they are just giving you false

hope on something or just giving you the

runaround. Some people's peace can be disrupted

when someone just comes along and gives you

false hope, but all the while they may have a hidden

agenda. I am not saying do not trust anybody

however, all I am saying is that be aware of what is

always going on around you.

It is just like I said before in a previous chapter that we must learn how to be selective of the people we may want to befriend. Even someone you may be close with can betray you and cause a distraction. The smaller your circle the better off you are because the fewer people that you deal with the chances of having more peace increases.

One way to avoid distraction when it comes to protecting your peace is to tackle one of your biggest priorities first. God should be everyone's number one priority first and foremost; we should pray every day and ask for forgiveness. When being a follower of Christ, there are some worldly challenges that we must overcome and be at peace. God does give us true rest when we follow and do his will.

Another way to avoid distractions when it comes to protecting your peace is to set boundaries. When setting boundaries, it is not that you are acting like you are better than the other people; it is more to it than that. The whole purpose of trying to protect your peace is to avoid stuff that may be either unnecessary or just stay away from people that may not have you best interest at heart. You may want to set boundaries on how people treat you for example, you do not have to put up with their disrespect towards you. People get mad and surprised when a person who is always calm and collected starts to set boundaries on how they want to be treated because the people who are disrespectful toward a person who is easygoing all the time realize that they do not have to put up with their negative energy.

Taking a break and be an effective way to avoid distractions. It is just like if you want to go on a trip to take time from work for example, you are not supposed to be thinking about anything but the activities that are involved with the trip that you may be taking. What I am trying to say when going on a trip is to act like you do not have any care in the world and have a great time.

We all need a break occasionally from life to have peace of mind and an escape from reality. Hard work does pay off. Life is hard enough as it is, but taking a break from the routine that you may follow every day can have some positive results depending on what you are doing. Remember when taking a trip somewhere always act like you do not

have a care in the world because you are escaping

reality for a while.

One of the last ways that I will be talking

about when it comes to avoiding distractions is

procrastination. Everybody always postpones

things because it is either they are too scared to

make it happen or do not know how to. When going

after our goals we must learn to first have peace of

mind when do so and avoid procrastinating all the

time. Sometimes when procrastinating we miss out

on stuff, that may be important in life. There is not

anything to be afraid of when either wanting peace

or going after your goals. Keep God first in all

things that you do, and you will not only be at

peace, but you will also have the confidence to

achieve any goal that you put your mind to. With

God by our side, all things are possible.

CHAPTER 24

Embrace your Solitude

The words solitude and peace go hand in

hand because most people like their solitude

because it is more peaceful. Solitude can also keep

you out of a lot of negative things that may come

your way. Some people prefer to be alone than to

be in a crowd full of people. I like my solitude

because it helps me focus on my goals and have

peace of mind.

Always embrace your solitude. You may be the one that people judge because you are different from them, but sometimes no company can be a good thing. Some people who do not have family come visit them often because they are either too busy or just do not want to reach out to you. When some people are so used to being alone, then it no longer bothers them if another person comes by the house besides it is more peaceful that way. The people that like their solitude sometimes have trouble making friend because they are worried about their peace being disturbed.

There is nothing wrong with embracing your solitude however, it can hinder you in a way that you may not want to interact with anyone just because you may like your peace a little more. I personally love my peace and quiet, but some company would be nice occasionally. Embracing your solitude can be also good for the soul.

I do remember being in a relationship that I had to tell my girlfriend at the time to bear with me because when you been single for so long you must get used to someone being around again. It took me a while to not be so alone and needed space all the time, and I learned how to be more outgoing and fun to be around instead of being boring.

Taking a step back for social media can be another way to enjoy your solitude. When you are working on your goals, the last thing you may need is drama that will distract you from them. I honestly feel that stay off social media can keep you out of trouble and help you stay focus on the goal you may want to achieve. I am not saying that we need to

stay off social media for good, but it is not a bad

idea to take a break occasionally.

It is also best to stay away from people that

like to be in the middle of drama that may be online.

There is more to life than being in the middle of

chaos and drama. That is why it is important to

embrace your solitude. Everyone needs to go

missing in action occasionally because it can also

help you have peace of mind.

I am going to use a break-up for example,

when a relationship comes to an end of course you

are heartbroken, sad, angry, and confused all at the

same time; but how you get through it would be

finding yourself again, don't try to find another

person right away, or just get yourself mind right

again so you can heal. Trying to heal from a long-

term relationship can be easier said than done. One

of the things that may hurt you the most is that the

person that you were with has moved on and may

not be thinking about you at all. God knows that if it

is meant to be then he or she will come back into

your life, however, do not wait around on them to

decide on rather they want to be with you or not.

When you are unloved let go. I know healing from a

relationship can be hard, but for your mind to be at

peace it must be done. Embracing your solitude is

also important, especially after a break-up.

Whether you and your partner get back together or

not, remember it is ok to be alone. When it is all

said and done God is in control at the end of the

day. Always embrace your solitude and praise God in the good and bad times.

Being alone and enjoying your solitude can help increase self-awareness. The definition of self-awareness is the ability to tune in your feelings, thoughts, and actions. Being able to recognize how other people see you. Self-aware people recognize their strengths and their challenges. When you are self-aware it makes you have an open mind about certain things in life and do not be so quick to jump to conclusion during certain situations.

CHAPTER 25

Spending Time with Nature

When spending time with nature it can mean a lot of things. Some people do this for various reasons; it can be from just taking a walk to just sitting down outside and meditating. I honestly think that everyone needs some form of escape no matter what it is. Life can be a challenge sometimes and one of the best ways to escape reality temporally is to spend some time outside.

It is also important to not take our freedom for granted because they are nothing like being free to go outside and enjoy what God has put on this Earth without anyone telling us what to do. I personally was I kid that liked going outside a lot because I felt like there was more to do besides staying in a house and playing video games all day. Times have changed and we see more kids on either a tablet or playing video games instead of being outside and enjoying the fresh air. When spending time with nature you will not only feel more at peace you will get to learn about nature a lot more.

One way that you can spend time with nature is to take walks either by yourself or with someone. Taking walks by yourself can also be what the doctor orders; it can calm you down and help you

escape. I remember reading the bible about Adam

and Eve walking with God during the cool of the

day; I thought that it was amazing for them to be

walking and talking with God. We still can walk and

talk with God rather we are going through good or

bad times.

When taking a walk in the park or anywhere

you want your mind to be at peace and not have a

care in the world. I know that it is easier said than

done especially when you either are in a

depression or just trying to get over a breakup.

There are some walks that we need to take alone

because being at peace with yourself is one of the

most important things your state of mind must be

in. Sometimes, just lying in the grass and looking at

the clouds can be peaceful. You can positively lose yourself when you start to just spend more time with nature than sitting in a house all day and just complaining about being bored.

Another way to spend time with nature would be observing your surroundings. Always be aware of your surrounding because you never know what is either going on or what could happen. Anything can happen at any given time. Being aware of what is going on when it comes to spending time with nature is one of the best traits to have. Paying attention to what is going on around you is a must because when your peace is be disturbed you should always keep your guard up at protect it at all costs.

CHAPTER 26

Knowing your Priorities in Life

Honestly, everyone's number one priority in life should be serving God; we all fall short of his glory daily, but he also gives us chances to follow him and be on his side. When having God as your number one priority, anything is possible. He also shows mercy and pardon for all his people by sending his son Jesus to die on the cross for our sins so we might be saved from going to hell.

The next thing that will be talked about is self-preservation. When it comes to maintaining your peace, you must learn how to get rid of the things that may be in your life that is causing the chaos. Some people love not having a lot of company but at the same time, they be longing for someone to come see them. I prefer peace over chaos any day of the week. The meaning of the word self-preservation is the protection of oneself from harm or death, especially regarded as a basic instinct in human beings and animals. Being able to figure out what your priorities are at a young age does has its advantages. You will get a heads up on how life is by trying to better yourself and keep your space and peace from being invaded by people that can be a negative influence in your life.

When knowing what your priorities are you can also feel less stress about certain things that may be going on in your life. You can also take care of certain situations accordingly without feeling stressed about it. I often hear people choosing peace over chaos because the more you react to the people who are ignorant about certain situations, the more stressed out you will be. You do not have to give anyone an explanation on why you chose not to react; that is when you start acting like an adult and just move on with your life.

I will use a couple that was in a relationship for example, do not mind me I am just speaking in general. You may have experienced a bad breakup,

and your heart is broken; you are also asking yourself why did he or she do this to me or what did I do wrong for this to happen. The truth is that we cannot make anyone be in our lives if they do not want to; for the people that are trying to cope with the fact that the person that they may have loved left them, especially for little or no reason, it is best to just move on and let go because if God wants you to be with that person they would not have left. It is just like what Denzel Washington said, "if you are rejected accept it, if you are unloved let go." Always know what your priorities are and take them head-on. Life is too short to be holding on to someone that has either betrayed your trust or broke your heart and they are just going on with their life like you don't even exist.

Move accordingly and someday you will get what you deserve because hard work and persistence pay off in the long run.

Taking responsibility on how you spend your time can be another way to finding out what your priorities are in life. Let's just say that you want to start a podcast I mean you have been talking about it for so long and procrastinating, but at the same time you are either lazy or doing something else that may not be productive in life; then one day you wake up a realize that for me to start this podcast I have to make it one of my priorities and stop doing other things that doesn't add value to my life.

When we start to learn to take responsibility for how we spend our time, then the more peaceful life can be. Let's just face it everyone wants to be at peace; however, we not only have to be at peace with ourselves, but we must also learn to maintain it as well. Do not feel bad for choosing peace over chaos. Always have God as your number one priority when it comes to maintaining your peace.

You can also waste a lot of time doing things that are not a priority in your life. When it comes down to make important decisions about priorities and boundaries stand on what you say by backing it up with action. Always stand on what you say and mean it. You cannot get mad at the results if you haven't put in the necessary work that may be required to achieve your goals in life.

CHAPTER 27

Working Things Out with People

When working things out with people in a

positive way, it can have some great results. Some

things can be fixed as well as others can be beyond

fixing depending on the problem or the situation. It

is just like is said before sometimes it is less

important to be right than it is to be at peace. Do

not let anything consume you as far as your anger

towards someone or an old grudge. When we start to learn how to communicate better with people, life will be a little more peaceful.

I recall having a disagreement with my mother and we were both upset at the time, but when we started to just sit down and talk about what was going on than we both came up with a solution to the issue that we both had. It is not good to jump to conclusions all the time when it comes to an issue or just about life in general. Learning to work things out when times get hard can be a challenge especially when it comes to an enemy, but when both parties have a common problem then it would be best if you all work together instead of arguing about something that may be irrelevant to the situation.

Protecting Your Peace by Any Means Necessary

You may be asking yourself how can working things out with people help keep the peace; well, I am going to just say this when we start to look at the bigger picture instead of just getting angry about little things, then your mind will be at peace instead or confusion. You never want to have your mind racing all the time. You also never want to hold on to hold grudges because when doing so your mind is not at peace and somebody is so-called living rent-free in your thoughts all the time. I refuse to let anyone, or anything destroy my mind or peace because we are all here on borrowed time and life is too short to be angry all the time just because of something that has happened in the past.

You cannot get yesterday back, what is done cannot be undone. It is best to make peace with your adversary and not hold on to an old grudge. I am not saying that you must be friends with them again, but what I am saying is that forgive them and move on with your life and live in peace because that is what God wants us to do, and it is the right thing. It is just like couples who are non-communitive and would rather leave a relationship instead of resolving the issues. Being in a relationship is not always going to be easy, people have their good and bad days, but when you are with a person for so long and they decide they want to leave you without resolving the issue and not communicate then they were never for you in the first place.

Protecting Your Peace by Any Means Necessary

Working things out will also protect your peace. Do not be part of the problem all the time standing in the background waiting for things to happen; you must be a part of the solution and make things happen. It is just like having a goal in life and you are not doing the necessary things to make it happen. You can have dreams, goals, and plans all you want but if you are not going to put in the work to make things happen then it doesn't mean anything.

When working things out with people you must encourage that the problems will be solved instead of doubting a person all the time. Peace can be protected when working together to solve problem because both parties have a common goal and wants to achieve success. No matter what the status is as far as both parties' friendship, do not

discourage each other because you both are trying

the accomplish a common goal together, and

maybe one day you do not have the be enemies

anymore.

CHAPTER 28

Love, Happiness, and Peace

Love, happiness, and peace are the things

that most people want when dealing with everyday

life. We must learn to take the good with the bad

and smile with the sad. We are going to have our

good and bad days; it is just how we learn to deal

with and cope with everyday life. some people want

to be negative all the time, but when you learn how

to love and forget how to hate then life can be so much easier.

You have some people in this world that love everyone and would give them the shirt off their back; you also have the one that will take advantage of good people without any regret at all. It is often said that you should love the people who love you however that is not the right way to think because God wants us to love everyone like it does whether you are friends with this person or not. All three of these words that are in the title of this chapter go hand in hand together because you basically cannot have one without the other. I will be describing the meaning of these words as well as how we can apply them into everyday life.

LOVE

The definition of the word love is an intense feeling of deep affection. Love can be a beautiful thing when everything is right in God's eyes. Love can bring you peace of mind as well however, it can be misused for manipulation or others that are just trying to do right by people. I always remembered my mother telling me that if it not out of love then it doesn't mean anything. Everybody wants to be loved in certain ways whether through friendships, relationships, or just having love for someone.

One of the reasons why love can be misused is because people can manipulate and gaslight you at the same time. That is one of the things that we need to watch out for as far as people misusing the

word love. Loving someone and being loved back in

return is one of the greatest feelings in the world

because they are not only saying it, but they are

also showing love and backing up what they mean

daily. The love that we have for our significant other

can be a great thing and never should be taken for

granted as far as a relationship is concerned.

Peace can also come from love because when the

feeling is mutual, the bond can be very strong.

HAPPINESS

Like the word love, happiness can also bring

you peace of mind. I understand that we cannot be

happy all the time; we will have our good and bad

days, but it is how we get through them. It is just

like Job in the bible, he learns to take the good with

the bad because God was testing him and no

matter what he kept his faith that he will get the job

done. Just like the word peace, we must learn to

protect our happiness as well. Some people do not

want to see you succeed or do better than them,

that includes family, friend, or even people you may

not know or have any contact with.

some people do not want to hear good new

when it comes to being happy because they either

do not have a life or just miserable all the time.

Misery loves company, and if we are not careful

with who we let in our inner circle then we can fall

right into that category with the people who are

angry and miserable all the time. Well, do not need

to let the devil take our joy from us because God expects us to be happy and to be happy for other people. For us to receive blessings from God, we must learn to clap for other people during their season. You will find peace of mind when you are happy and can focus on your goals.

The words solace and happiness can also go hand in hand as well. When we usually find solace in something we love to do, we are happy about it. It is also up to us whether we want to live and protect our peace by being happy or just create chaos and malice wherever we go. Being happy with what you have teaches us how to be contempt while working for what we want.

Never try to destroy someone else happiness because you are miserable because at the end of the day, you reap what you sow. Be happy for the people that may be doing better than you in life because you never know what type of things that they may have gone through to get where they are. Some people struggle worse than others to achieve their goals and will not let anything stand in the way of their happiness that may have eluded them for so long.

Some people can sense that someone or something coming from a mile away to destroy their happiness; that is why they have a select few friends that understand their point of view. We are all growing up in an age where we want stability and happiness, however for that to happen we must make sacrifices when it comes to protecting and maintaining our peace. Do not argue with people when you know you are right because it is just like

debating with a stop sign. We do not have to react

to every bad situation when it comes to maintaining

our peace because it that is done then we become

part of the problem instead of the solution.

PEACE

When it comes to the word peace, there are

sacrifices that need to be make for us to have it in

our life. When having peace of mind, you are happy

and able to love people in general. Also, when it

comes to loving someone, we must learn to love

ourselves first. It is just like God loves us so must

that he gave his only some to die for us so we may

have eternal life; he also wants us to live our lives

in peace however, we all fall short of the lord's

glory daily. Remember, for us to be happy in life we

must also have the peace of mind and protect it at

all costs. Do not be envious of anyone's success

because your time is coming, just wait on God.

CHAPTER 29

Tending to your Own Business

When we start to become mature in life, it is best to mind our own business because it is another way to protect our peace. You never want to be labeled as a busybody especially when you come to cause chaos and create malice wherever you go. You can also find solace when you tend to your own business because when people try to say that you were involved in something bad, you can verify that you weren't.

There are many ways to be about your business; it can be from just making your own money or just completing projects. It is just like Jesus when he was twelve years old that he was preaching in the temple, and he told his earthly parents that he was about his father's business which was God himself. When you are minding your own business, you are also protecting your peace. It is not good to be in everyone else's business when it comes to gossiping about someone; I mean we are all guilty of it from time to time however, we must try to keep that at a minimum.

It is just like that old saying, if you can't say anything nice don't say anything at all. There is a lot of truth behind that saying because when you are always constantly talking about someone in a negative way, you are either miserable or have no life whatsoever. It is best to help people when they are struggling rather, he or she is your friend or foe. You owe anybody the time ow day because you never truly know what they may be going through in life. Sometimes, one of the only ways to keep the peace is to not say anything at all about someone else's business when they have trusted you not to tell anybody what is going on.

When it comes to understanding how to tend to your own business you must learn not to jump into every conversation you hear. When you start to make it a habit of not participating in every conversation, you can not only maintain your peace, but you can also save yourself a lot of grief. We all want to live a happy and peaceful life, but it comes with sacrifices because when you are not jumping into everyone's conversation or just being a busy body, you tend to miss out on so called juicy information about certain people.

They say that it is not good to tell your business to everyone, but at the same time it also not good to know everyone else's; the reason why I say that is because that is how rumor get started. There are three sides to every story the two parties that are involved and the truth. We are all guilty when it comes to eavesdropping in other people's business from time to time, but you don't want to make a habit of doing that.

There are also times when people take whatever a person say about another and run with it without knowing the facts; we are all guilty of that as well. When we get older and start to mature as adults most people want to be a part of the solution instead of the problem because most people do not have the time for drama, chaos, or malice. They want to find and protect their peace by finding solace in something that they may like to do as a hobby and staying out of the way.

When living a life of solitude, it can get lonely at the top so to speak, however over time you tend to embrace it by staying out of the way. It is best sometimes to stay out of the way because sometimes the less you know about a person's business the better off you can be. When you start to stay to yourself a lot more, it can pay dividends. I

am not saying it is a bad thing to conversate with

anyone, but just be careful who you talk about

because you never know who that person knows

especially when they may be friends with your

enemy.

Chapter 30

Final Thoughts

Well, I am going to tell you about my final thoughts about keeping and maintaining your peace. Having a peaceful mindset on things is very important because it can help you think more logically and clear. Sometimes we let certain people in our lives that may not have our best interests at heart; that is why when you become a child of God that you start to separate yourself from people like that. Not everybody that we meet are meant to stay in our lives.

We must learn that it is ok to love someone from a distance and move on with our lives because if you keep holding on to that person that doesn't care about either your feelings or you as a person it can drive you insane. I always said this to myself, I will personally leave a person alone if they don't want to be bothered with me anymore; do not get things twisted just because I leave a person alone doesn't mean that I will let them come back in my life and disturb my peace again. Self-preservation kicks in when the person you love is not respecting you as for me, I will take respect over love any day of the week. In general, going through a breakup is bad but it is even worse when you haven't done anything for it to happen. Never let your past dictate your future because if you haven't moved on from either a person that you may have been in love with, then you cannot have a future with someone else.

I am not an expert on anything that I have talked about in this book; I am just going off my personal experience in my long journey in this life. I do not know what God's plan is for me when it comes to my life but at the end of the day he is in control. God has someone for everyone, but we must learn to be at peace with him first and foremost and be patient.

Always say what you feel and mean what you say. Setting boundaries, learning how to tell people no, and telling people the truth about what you may be feeling in the moment are just three of many

ways to maintain and protect your peace at all

costs. Never regret saying what is on your mind

even if it costs you friends or relationships; you do

not have to deal with people disrespecting you all

the time because how a person treats you whether

it is good or bad is how they feel about you. Certain

people will test your inner peace daily. Sometimes,

we must get out of character for us to get our point

across because they weren't trying to listen to you

when being nice about it, but when you get out of

character, they want to call you crazy.

I honestly do not like my peace to be

disturbed especially when it comes to somebody

that you think will stay in your life and suddenly,

they leave. We cannot make anyone stay in our life

but what we can do is move on from them and become the best version of ourselves. I can love and forgive you from a distance, and at the same time I can also leave you alone when it comes to protecting my peace.

We also cannot be afraid to be alone. When being real and honest all the time you are going to have very few friends. You do not have to fight for respect when it comes to a relationship because sooner or later something has got to give; and what I mean is that walking away from a bad relationship can bring you peace of mind as well, however it can hurt for a while but once you start to feel like you can live without this person you can truly move on and be at peace. When a person doesn't feel appreciated in a relationship rather male or female, they will give you a version of themselves that they can survive in, and you will not like that version at all. It is just like you can do and do for a person and no matter what they are never satisfied, but when you stop doing them things that you normally do for them, they should be worried; the thing is that they have chosen peace over chaos, and they are protecting it by any means necessary.

It is like I said before life is too short not to be at peace or be happy. We cannot be at peace when our mind is full of negative thoughts. We must learn to think positively and have an open mind about things. Life is not easy; you will have your stumbling blocks in front of you.

The last thought I will discuss when it comes to protecting your peace will be finding solace. The words solace and peace go hand in hand because

when you find solace in something that you love to

do then peace is found also. I find solace when it

comes to writing about certain subjects that can

relate to life. I am not saying that I am the best

when it comes to giving good advice because we all

fail at some point when it comes to practicing what

we are preaching; face it we are human, and we are

going to make mistakes. Finding solace in

something can be beautiful, especially when it

comes to keeping the peace and having a positive

mindset. Remember, keep God first and all things

will fall into place, and I hope and pray that

everyone will find peace in their lives, and

remember to protect it by any means necessary. Do

not go to bed mad or upset because you never

know; keep that positive mindset, put God first in everything you do in life, and praise him in good and bad times.

Well until next time; keep it real, live life happy, and protect your peace at all costs.

God bless you all.

THE END

"Trust God in anything and everything you do in life: follow him and he will always be with you."

ABOUT THE AUTHOR

I am just a laid back guy from a small town in Missouri that is trying to do big things. You never want to become a prisoner of your past because you will never have peace of mind that is why I wrote this book to get the word out there. I am also a person that likes his solitude however, I do not mind company at all a welcome anyone that want to come in my life in a positive way; I can feel it when a person's intentions are not good. When I start to feel like people are trying to destroy my peace then I set that boundary and let them go on about their business; don't get me wrong I treat them nice, but I was always taught to be very observant because you do not know what they may be capable of. For the people who know me, I try to treat people the way I want to be treated.

Take Care

Jerrell A. Gooden

Another thing that I would like to add is that I refuse to be one of these men that feels like that i only have responsibilities instead of rights; I have a right to be happy, sad, or upset. I have always kept my emotions to myself in fear of not being heard but that has started to change as the years are going by. Do not get me wrong I do consider other's feelings before I say something however, I am all about protecting my peace no matter what I must do.

It is not good to keep things inside of you when you are hurting. We also have a right to express ourselves when we are feeling some type of way. always remember to exercise your rights as a human being to express yourself and also be careful with who you vent to because you can't trust just anyone in life because they may not have your best interest at heart.

"Always remember to make the most of every day, and praise God during the good and bad times."

LIVE IN PEACE

www.ingramcontent.com/pod-product-compliance
Lightning Source LLC
Chambersburg PA
CBHW072346090426
42741CB00012B/2941